The California
Condor

Other titles in the Returning Wildlife series include:

The American Alligator
The Bald Eagle
Bats
The Florida Panther
Green Sea Turtles
Gray Wolves
Grizzly Bears
Manatees
The North American Beaver
The North American Bison
North American River Otters
Wild Turkeys

Returning Wildlife

The California
Condor

John E. Becker

KIDHAVEN
PRESS™

THOMSON

GALE

San Diego • Detroit • New York • San Francisco • Cleveland
New Haven, Conn. • Waterville, Maine • London • Munich

To Bill Dennler, who appreciates the true beauty of vultures

Picture Credits:
Cover: © F.K. Truslow/VIREO
© Bettmann/CORBIS, 8, 16 (inset)
© Jonathan Blair/CORBIS, 19
© Tom Brownold, 37
CDC, 20
© David Clendenen/USFWS, 9, 10, 26, 35
© W. Perry Conway/CORBIS, 10 (inset)
© CORBIS, 7
© COREL Corporation, 16, 20 (inset)
© Richard Cummins/CORBIS, 15
© Ron Garrison/San Diego Zoo/USFWS, 31, 32 (inset), 33
Greenhaven Press, 13
Greenhaven Press/USFWS, 28
© Gary Kramer/USFWS, 22, 24 (inset)
Library of Congress, 17
© Marc Muench/CORBIS, 24
© PhotoDisc, 34, 38-39
© Joel Sartore / www.joelsartore.com, 27, 32
© F.K. Truslow/VIREO, 39 (inset)
USFWS, 11

For more information, contact
KidHaven Press
27500 Drake Rd.
Farmington Hills, MI 48331-3535
Or you can visit our Internet site at http://www.gale.com

LIBRARY OF CONGRESS CATALOGING-IN-PUBLICATION DATA

Becker, John E., 1942-
  The California Condor / by John E. Becker.
    v. cm. — (Returning wildlife)
  Summary: Discusses the history, characteristics, behavior, and habitat of the California condor, including population decline, conservation efforts, and recovery. Includes bibliographical references (p.   ).
    ISBN 0-7377-2292-4 (hardback : alk. paper)
  1. California Condor—Juvenile literature. [1. California Condor. 2. Condors. 3. Endangered species.] I. Title. II. Series.

Printed in the United States of America

Contents

Chapter One 6
    Giant Birds

Chapter Two 14
    A Long Decline

Chapter Three 22
    California Condors Return

Chapter Four 30
    Looking to the Future

Glossary 41

For Further Exploration .42

Index 45

Acknowledgments 47

About the Author 48

chapter 1

Giant Birds

Centuries ago, condors flew across much of western North America as well as areas in the south and east. By the 1840s, most condors were found only along the Pacific coast of California.

Over the next one hundred years, California condors steadily declined in numbers as their habitat disappeared and people killed them. By the middle of the twentieth century, about two dozen California condors remained.

In the 1980s, those birds were taken from the wild and placed in zoos, where they produced chicks. Those **captive-bred** chicks were successfully released back into their natural habitat, and there is now reason to believe that they may survive into the future.

Age-Old Birds

Condors have been soaring over the skies of North America for more than 13 million years. Some huge condors, which are now extinct, once lived in North America. *Teratornis incredibilis,* for example, had a wingspan of almost twenty feet. Ancient condors fed on the **carcasses** of gigantic mammals that roamed the earth, such as mammoths, saber-toothed cats, giant sloths, and giant beavers.

California condors are closely related to these ancient birds. They are members of a family of birds known as New World vultures, and they are related to other vultures such as turkey vultures and black vultures. California condors are most closely related, however, to Andean condors of South America, which have a ten-foot wingspan.

California condors first appeared more than forty thousand years ago. Many condor bones from that time have been found in the La Brea tar pits in Los Angeles, California. California condors fed on the gigantic mammals that lived across North America. About ten thousand years ago, however, most of the gigantic mammals died out. Thereafter, California condors were found only

A zookeeper uses a puppet to feed a condor chick. A number of condor chicks raised in captivity have been successfully released into the wild.

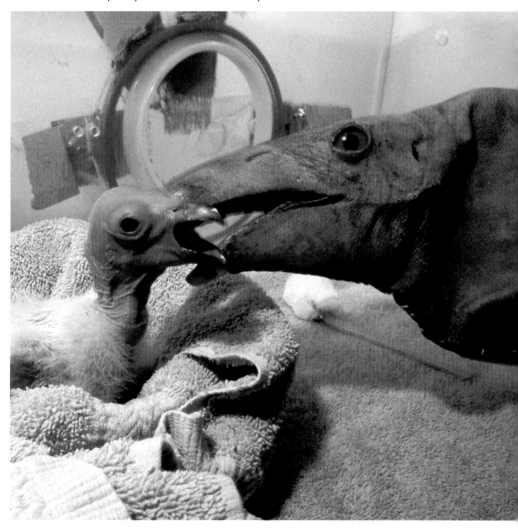

Ancient condors, relatives of the California condor, perch on a tree as saber-toothed cats prowl below.

in the western portions of North America, where they survived by feeding on large sea creatures that had died and washed ashore.

Distinctive Birds

California condors are the largest soaring land birds in North America. An adult California condor may weigh up to twenty-five pounds and have a wingspan of nine and a half feet. California condors, like other vultures, have no feathers on their heads. They are bald from the neck up, and their naked heads are orange red in color. Condor feathers are black, except for a distinctive triangle of white on the underside of each wing. Adult California condors have glittery red eyes.

Nature's Cleanup Crew

California condors play an extremely important role in nature. They remove the remains of dead animals. If not for condors and other vultures, rotting animal carcasses, or **carrion**, might litter the land, spreading diseases to animals and people. Condors are well suited for their role.

Condors have long, sharp, powerful beaks that allow them to tear open the tough hides of the large, dead mammals they eat. A condor may eat three or four pounds of meat at a time, storing the food in a pouch below its throat called a crop. It may not eat again for several days.

Condors hear quite well. Scientists discovered that California condors were able to hear loud noises over a

Condors feed on the flesh of dead animals, known as carrion. Here, captive-bred condors devour an animal carcass.

mile away. They also have extremely good eyesight. California condors have been known to change their behavior if they spot a person within five hundred yards (the length of five football fields). Their keen eyesight also allows them to see dead animals from the great heights at which they soar.

Behaviors

Condors soar across the sky on warm air currents that provide updrafts known as **thermals**. They have been observed soaring for hours as they scan the landscape

The condor's excellent hearing and keen eyesight help it find food and spot predators up to five hundred yards away.

below, searching for dead animals. Because condors feed together, scientists believe that they may circle over a dead animal to signal other condors that food is available. Condors are capable of flying faster than fifty-five miles per hour and may reach as high as fifteen thousand feet (the same height that some airplanes fly). Condors have also been known to travel great distances while **foraging** for food. They may cover as much as 150 miles in a single day.

California condors do not migrate with the change of seasons, as many other birds do. Condors usually establish a home range and crisscross that area searching for food. If food becomes scarce in one area, the condors will establish new territory. They will remain in that territory as long as food can be found.

California condors will **roost**, nest, and feed near other condors. They return to the same roosting sites year after year. Like other highly social animals, they have a definite social structure based on dominance. **Dominant** birds will have first choice at roosting and nesting sites as well as at feeding sites. Older, more dominant birds will always be given the first chance to eat at a carcass.

Condors appear to be quite intelligent. They are also extremely curious and may even approach people out of curiosity. Young condors have been observed engaging in spirited play. They can entertain themselves with grass, sticks, feathers, and other objects for long periods of time.

When mating season arrives, male condors perform a courtship ritual for the females. During the courtship dance, the male stands with his wings partly held open, his head held down, and his neck arched forward as he slowly turns and rocks from side to side. California condors also perform graceful moves in the air during mating season.

Reproduction

California condors reach breeding age between six and seven years of age. They will generally stay with the same mate for life unless one of the pair dies. In that event, the surviving condor will seek a new mate.

Breeding generally takes place between December and spring. Once condors have mated, they nest in secluded locations. Caves in the face of steep cliffs appear to be the favorite spot for most condors. Other nesting choices include tree cavities near the top of tall trees or in hard-to-reach rock ledges. Condors do not build a nest from tree branches but may move small rocks to form a nest.

Female condors usually lay a single, pale-blue egg between March and mid-May. The eggs may reach five inches in length. If the egg is broken or taken by predators, the condor pair may produce a second egg. Both parents will take turns sitting on the egg to **incubate** it. A chick will hatch from the egg from fifty-four to fifty-eight days after the egg is laid. Both parents care for and feed the chick.

About six months after hatching, the chick's flight feathers will develop to the point that it may begin flying. The chick may depend on its parents for as much as a year and a half after it begins flying and learning to find food and feed on its own in the wild.

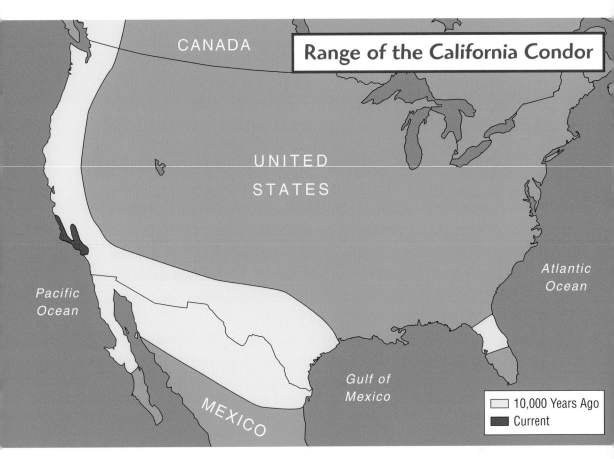

Range of the California Condor

CANADA

UNITED
STATES

Pacific
Ocean

Atlantic
Ocean

MEXICO

Gulf of
Mexico

☐ 10,000 Years Ago
■ Current

Scientists believe that condors are able to live long lives. Condors have not been studied long enough to know for certain how long they live. Some experts believe they may live forty to sixty years in the wild.

Habitat

For California condors to live that long, however, they need large, open areas with plenty of food. Their habitat must be able to support the large mammals that they depend on for food. The ideal condor habitat also includes air currents that are favorable for thermals so the condors can soar. As people move into remote areas, condor habitat is shrinking. Loss of habitat has been one factor in the decline of California condors.

chapter 2

A Long Decline

For centuries, California condors maintained small but constant populations along the Pacific coast of North America. Their territory stretched from British Columbia in Canada to the Baja Peninsula in Mexico. The condors in California at that time fed on whales and seals that sometimes washed ashore. Large herds of pronghorn antelope, elk, and mule deer that flourished in California's Central Valley added to the plentiful supply of food.

The Native Americans who lived in this area for thousands of years believed that the birds had magical powers. Many tribes felt a strong spiritual bond with condors. Though they killed some of the birds for religious ceremonies, no one knows for sure how this affected condor populations.

Early Visitors

Europeans arrived on the Pacific coast in the seventeenth century, followed by American explorers two hundred years later. It was during this time that the condor population began its long, steady decline.

The first Europeans to visit the Pacific coast of North America were the Spanish. When Spanish priest Father Antonio de la Ascension sailed with an expedition into Monterey Bay in central California in 1602, he observed huge birds soaring in the sky. He described the birds as they gathered on the beach to feed on the carcass of a whale that had washed ashore. Those birds were California condors. Father de la Ascension and his fellow explorers are the first known Europeans to observe condors in North America.

Two hundred years later, American explorers Meriwether Lewis and William Clark traveled along the Columbia River in present-day Washington State. Their journals include detailed sketches and descriptions of condors.

No one knows for certain what started the condor's decline. Early European and American visitors probably killed some of them. And condor numbers also dropped as settlers moved into their territory. But the worst threats to condor populations were yet to come.

Beginning about 1840, condors disappeared from one area after another. By 1850, condors were almost

More than four hundred years ago Spanish explorers observed condors soaring above the California coast.

American explorers Meriwether Lewis and William Clark (left) described seeing condors along Washington State's Columbia River (above) in the 1800s.

completely gone from the Washington and Oregon Territories. They disappeared in Arizona by the early 1920s. The last California condors were gone from Baja California in Mexico in the 1930s. By the 1940s, the range of the California condor had shrunken to a U-shaped area that extended from the coast near Monterey, California, to just north of Los Angeles and back up to the inland area around Tulare County in central California.

Settlers Move West

There were many different reasons for the decline of California condors. The California gold rush in 1849 attracted thousands of fortune seekers to the Far West. Some of those gold miners found enough gold to buy land and

The California gold rush of 1849 brought many settlers to the West. These settlers killed many California condors.

establish ranches with large herds of cattle and other domestic animals. Ranchers and hunters killed the wild animals that competed with their livestock for grazing range. When cows, sheep, or other ranch animals died, condors would often feed on the carcasses. In the mistaken belief that condors were killing their livestock, ranchers shot many of the birds.

American settlers also shot or poisoned them. Researchers believe only five hundred to a thousand California condors survived by the close of the nineteenth century.

As the giant vultures became increasingly scarce, **specimens** were in demand for displays in scientific collections in museums. Both amateur and professional collectors scoured the West in search of condors. Many condors and their large eggs were sold to museums for a handsome profit.

Sport hunters also targeted California condors, and without laws to protect them, many condors were shot. Unregulated hunting and egg collecting were the cause of many condor deaths.

Poison

Another threat emerged in the late 1800s. Government-supported programs to wipe out livestock predators such as coyotes led to accidental poisoning of condors. Poison was used to kill coyotes. Because California condors eat dead animals, many died from eating the poisoned meat.

A similar problem came up after World War II. An **insecticide** was introduced to help control insect pests on farms and in cities across the country. That product,

As condors became increasingly scarce at the close of the nineteenth century, museums began to collect specimens of the bird.

DDT (right), a poison used for decades to control insects (above), killed many large animals, including California condors.

DDT, was effective in killing insects, but birds and small animals ate the poisoned insects. Larger animals then ate the birds and small animals that had high levels of DDT in their bodies. DDT was soon found in animals throughout the food chain. Birds of prey such as bald eagles began declining in numbers as DDT caused problems in their ability to produce healthy offspring. California condors also suffered from the effects of eating dead animals contaminated with DDT.

Other Problems

By 1965, the California condor was nearing extinction. Scientists at that time estimated that only sixty survived. The steady loss of California condors and the very real possibility that they might become extinct caused great concern in the scientific community.

Yet another factor in the loss of condors was the tremendous growth in human populations in California during the second half of the twentieth century. Human population increases led to the growth of large cities across condor habitat. Loss of habitat, therefore, also became a factor in the decline of the species.

With so few California condors left in the wild, every bird seemed to matter. After three condors were found dead of lead poisoning from eating other animals that had been shot by hunters using lead bullets, the species seemed to be headed toward extinction. By 1982, only twenty-two condors remained in the wild.

The slow rate at which California condors reproduce added to the problems. Condors usually have a single offspring every other year, and they must be at least six years of age before they can begin producing chicks. So, condors replace themselves very slowly compared to other animals. This means it takes condors much longer to recover from population declines than other species.

Desperate Situation

The combined effect of all these factors made the prospects for saving the species quite remote. The survival of California condors reached a critical point in 1985 when six wild condors mysteriously disappeared. The missing condors included four individuals from the remaining five known breeding pairs. The survival of California condors as a species seemed unlikely. It would require desperate measures if condors were to be saved.

chapter 3

California Condors Return

Two biologists from the U.S. Fish and Wildlife Service (FWS) completed the difficult climb to an observation point in the rugged foothills of the Sespe Condor Sanctuary in Ventura County, California. They quickly unpacked their gear. As one of the biologists scanned the sky with his binoculars, the other held up an antenna and tuned a radio receiver to a predetermined frequency.

Suddenly the first biologist cried out, "There, over the valley!"

"Yes, that's number ninety-eight," replied the other biologist. "I've got a good, strong signal from him."

They had spotted one of the rarest animals in the world—a free-flying California condor.

A short while later, the biologists climbed to another vantage point and made an even more exciting observation. Across the valley in a small cave in the sheer rock face, a female condor, number 111, preened a fluffy condor chick. As the biologists watched the chick, they were encouraged to see that it appeared strong and healthy. Other chicks have been born to condors in these mountains since condors were returned to the wild in 1992. Unfortunately, all the other chicks have died. If this chick lives, then others may live as well, and California condors may yet survive.

Early Attempts to Learn About Condors

The first person to recognize that California condors were in serious trouble was **ornithologist** James G. Cooper.

After observing California condors for thirty-five years, Cooper concluded that they were heading toward extinction in 1890.

Over the next seventy-five years, various scientists tried to learn more about these little-known birds and why they were dying off. Cyril Robinson, the deputy supervisor of the Los Padres National Forest, and businessman Robert Easton began a five-year study in 1933.

California condor number ninety-eight preens its feathers in the Sespe Condor Sanctuary in Ventura County, California.

They surveyed California condors in the national forests of Southern California. That study indicated that possibly as few as sixty condors were surviving in an ever smaller area.

It was during this time period that Americans were beginning to view the loss of wildlife species with alarm. The Robinson-Easton study caused government

Los Padres National Forest (pictured) and other Southern California wilderness areas are home to condors (inset).

agencies to take action to protect California condors. In 1937, the U.S. Forest Service established a twelve-hundred-acre California condor sanctuary in the Sisquoc Falls area of Santa Barbara County. The sanctuary was established to protect condor wilderness habitat and to prevent people from getting close enough to be a threat to the condors.

In 1939, wildlife biologist Carl Koford began another long-term study of California condors. His work gave scientists more information about the biology and habits of the species. Even before the study concluded, Koford's findings led to the creation of the Sespe Wildlife Area (renamed the Sespe Condor Sanctuary in 1966) in 1947. The thirty-five-thousand-acre sanctuary represented an important step in efforts to prevent the extinction of condors. It protected condor habitat and helped prevent disturbance of condors by people. The National Audubon Society published the results of Koford's study in 1953. One of the strongest recommendations in the report was that additional protection be given to condors.

Greater Protective Measures

Condor populations continued to decline despite the establishment of sanctuaries. By 1964, only about forty California condors survived—twenty fewer than just eleven years earlier.

Added protection for condors was also provided through laws. In California, anyone convicted of shooting a condor could be fined up to one thousand dollars and sent to jail for up to one year. The federal government also passed the Endangered Species Act (ESA) in 1973. This law provided legal protection for many species, including condors. Killing, possessing, harming, or disturbing condors was a crime punishable under the ESA.

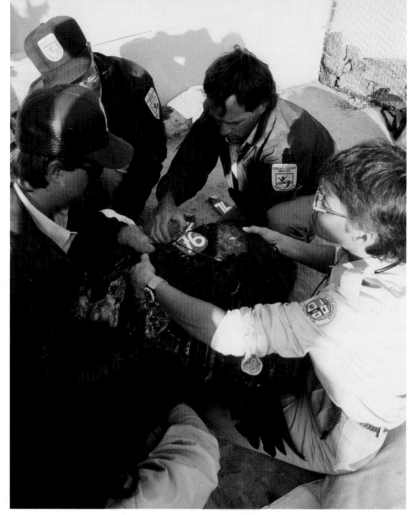

Scientists fit a California condor with a radio tag before releasing the animal back into the wild.

The Battle over How to Save Condors

The FWS felt that it had to do more, however. Condor experts feared that condor populations had fallen to a point from which they might not be able to recover. So, in 1979 the FWS announced a controversial plan to capture all remaining wild condors and place them in captivity. The plan also called for the development of a captive-breeding program aimed at building up the numbers of condors. Some of the condors produced by the breeding program would be fitted with **radio tags** and released back into the wild. The plan was opposed by a number of conservation organizations. Those organizations believed that the birds were too sensitive to be captured. They felt the stress of being handled might cause the remaining condors to die.

Wildlife officials decided to test their idea first on two close relatives of the California condor, black vultures and Andean condors. Neither of these were endangered. Several were captured and bred in captivity. They responded well. In 1981, four captive-bred Andean condors were released successfully in South America. By that time, the California program was ready to begin. The California Fish and Game Commission approved the capture, radio tagging, and captive breeding of the remaining California condors. The program got off to a slow start

These California condors are part of the Los Angeles Zoo's captive-breeding program.

chapter 4

Looking to the Future

It is early in the morning and the sun is already warming the cool, dry air as keepers begin their workday at the Los Angeles Zoo. A feeling of anticipation fills the air. Two of the worlds' most endangered animals, a pair of adult California condors, are about to take over the final stage of producing a condor chick. For fifty-three days, the condors have been sitting on a wooden egg while zookeepers have warmed their real egg in an incubator. Because they have been bred in captivity, they may not know how to properly care for the egg. By substituting a wooden egg, zookeepers ensure that the parents continue their incubation routine. They also give the chick a better chance of developing correctly.

When the condor parents leave the nest box, the keepers remove the wooden egg and replace it with the real one. Once the parents return to the nest box, they sit on the egg and continue incubating it naturally. Keepers using television cameras observe the entire process.

The next morning, keepers eagerly peek in on the egg after the parents leave. They are trying to see if the chick has pipped, or cracked the egg for the first time.

One of the keepers whispers, "I see the egg and it has a crack!"

Soon the crack becomes an opening, and the beak of the small, fluffy condor chick pokes out. Over the next three days, the chick continues to crack its shell until it finally breaks out.

Keepers remove the first egg laid by a female, and sometimes even the second egg, so the female condor may produce as many as three eggs in a season. That allows her to produce two or three times as many eggs as she would normally. The last egg stays with the parents, who will feed and raise the chick.

Zoo staff will raise the first and second chicks. They use hand puppets that look like adult condors to feed

A zookeeper checks a California condor egg that is being warmed in an incubator.

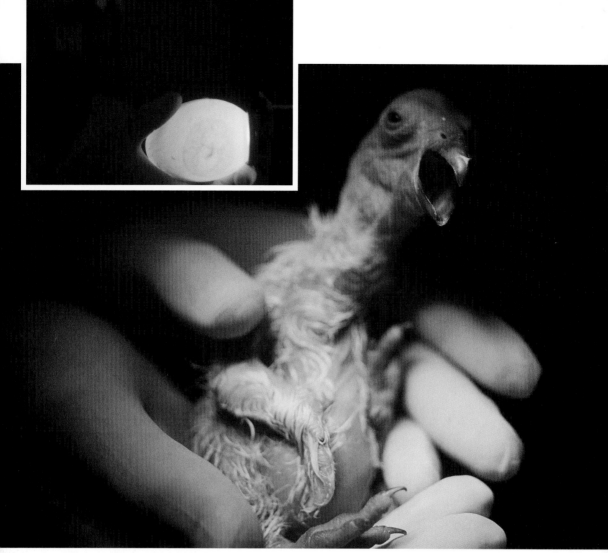

A condor chick (shown) develops inside the egg (inset) for about fifty-four days before hatching.

the chicks. The puppets ensure that the chicks do not confuse humans with their parents. Techniques such as these have been quite successful. Nine out of every ten chicks that have been born in captivity have survived.

Hazards Remain

Although there is reason to be optimistic about California condors, a number of hazards still threaten their survival. While condors are soaring and searching for dead animals below, they may not notice power lines. Hitting a power line may cause serious injury or death from electrocution. In the first few years after captive-bred condors were released into the wild, five of those birds died after colliding with power lines.

Zookeepers use a puppet that looks like an adult condor to feed a captive-bred condor chick.

Man-made hazards such as power lines pose a serious threat to California condors.

To do away with that problem, power poles have been placed in the flight pens of young condors that are being prepared for release. The poles give off a minor electrical shock, teaching the condors to avoid power lines and poles in the wild. This strategy has been successful in reducing deaths from power-line mishaps.

Another serious problem for California condors is lead poisoning from lead bullets. In the summer of 2000, five condors that had been released in Arizona died of lead poisoning after eating animals killed with lead shotgun pellets. A promising solution to this problem is the development of a bullet that is not poisonous to wild animals. Use of the new bullets, however, is voluntary, and it may be several years before their use is widespread.

Poaching presents another hazard for condors. People who want to boast of killing a rare animal sometimes hunt California condors. Because condors are such large birds, they represent an easy target. After California condors were released in the Grand Canyon area of Arizona, one of the birds was shot. The poacher was arrested and

A group of condors feeds on a dead animal. Many condors have died from eating animals killed with lead bullets.

prosecuted for killing a member of an endangered species. Unfortunately, many poachers are never caught.

Into the Future

Because of the slow rate at which California condors reproduce, captive breeding to build up condor numbers has been made the top priority for the recovery of the species. The Los Angeles Zoo, the San Diego Wild Animal Park, and the Peregrine Fund's World Center for Birds of Prey have all successfully produced condor chicks for release into the wild. The Los Angeles Zoo and the San Diego Wild Animal Park have been involved in the captive-breeding program from the beginning. Each of these two programs has produced over one hundred chicks.

The goal of the California Condor Recovery Plan is to establish a total of five captive-breeding sites. Those sites should produce enough chicks that the species may be taken off the endangered species list one day. A fourth captive-breeding program is getting under way at the Oregon Zoo in Portland. The zoo hopes to add six breeding pairs of condors to those already producing chicks for **reintroduction** to the wild.

Another major focus is the protection of natural habitat. Much of the land that has been set aside for the protection of condors in California is within state and federal wildlife refuges. The FWS manages the National Wildlife Refuge System, which includes Hopper Mountain National Wildlife Refuge in Southern California. That refuge consists of almost twenty-five hundred acres of rugged mountains, forests, and grasslands. Condors have lived in this area for centuries, so it was a natural location for reintroduction efforts. Several condor releases have taken place at the Hopper Mountain site. Condors that soar above the refuge are part of a program that has

A captive condor spreads its wings inside a Los Angeles Zoo enclosure.

been carried on since condors were first released there in 1992. Captive-bred condors, released in the wild, have now produced chicks in a nesting area close to the Hopper Mountain Refuge.

Expanding the number of release sites for captive-bred condors is another goal of the California Condor Recovery Plan. Currently there are three release sites in

California. Wildlife officials would like to have others in case any of the existing release sites become unusable.

Plans also call for private conservation organizations to continue their role in condor release programs. The Ventana Wilderness Society, for example, runs a holding area for California condors awaiting release in the Big Sur region of central California. The organization also has responsibility for reintroducing those condors back into the wild.

The Grand Canyon (pictured) is the focus of condor conservation efforts in Arizona. At right, condors perch on a tree near Big Sur, one of three condor release sites in California.

In Arizona, the release of California condors has been focused in the Grand Canyon area. The Peregrine Fund, another private wildlife conservation organization, runs the release program there. Because this program has been so successful, the Peregrine Fund has recommended expanding the boundaries for reintroduced condors. The boundaries could include southwestern Colorado and the entire states of Arizona, Utah, and New Mexico.

A Future for Condors

Today there are 80 California condors living in the wild and more than 140 living in captive-breeding facilities. In addition, one California condor chick was born in the wild in California and another in Arizona during the 2003 nesting season. These two events are extremely important. The California condor recovery program will be truly successful only when the condors are producing offspring naturally in the wild. There can be no question that the species has made a remarkable comeback. Now it is up to people to continue to help condors recover fully.

captive breeding: The breeding of animals held in captive facilities such as zoos.

carcass: A dead animal's body.

carrion: The flesh of a dead animal.

DDT: Dichlorodiphenyltrichloroethane, a chemical compound used to kill insects.

dominant: The highest ranking member of a group that controls the other members of the group.

forage: To search for food.

incubate: To keep eggs warm so that they will hatch.

insecticide: A chemical used to kill insect pests.

ornithologist: A scientist who studies birds.

radio tags: A radio-wave sending device attached to an animal.

reintroduce: To introduce again, as in returning animals to areas from which they disappeared.

roost: A resting place for birds.

specimen: A sample that represents an entire group.

thermal: An uplifting current of warm air.

Books

Caroline Arnold, *On the Brink of Extinction.* New York: Gulliver Green Books, 1993. Tale of the loss of California condors due to man's activities and the heroic efforts of numerous governmental agencies, zoos, and conservation organizations to prevent the extinction of the species.

Patricia A. Fink Martin, *California Condors.* New York: Childrens Press, 2002. Tells the story of the California condors' natural history, endangerment, and return to the wild with the help of people.

Nancy T. Schorsch, *Saving the Condor.* New York: Franklin Watts, 1991. The story of the struggle to prevent the extinction of California condors through captive breeding and the return of these large vultures to the wild.

Alvin Silverstein, Virginia Silverstein, and Laura Silverstein Nunn, *The California Condor.* Brookfield, CT: Millbrook Press, 1998. Describes the physical characteristics and behaviors of California condors, the circumstances leading to their decline, and the efforts to recover the species.

Periodical

San Francisco Chronicle, "Endangered Species Facing Tough Times, Study Says," December 6, 1996. The story relates the disappointing number of plant and animal species listed as endangered that are recovering. One of the returning species, however, is the California condor.

Organizations to Contact

Arizona Game and Fish Department
3500 S. Lake Mary Rd.
Flagstaff, AZ 86001

(928) 774-5045

www.gf.state.az.us

The governmental agency in the state of Arizona that is responsible for reintroducing California condors to that state.

The Los Angeles Zoo and Botanical Gardens

5333 Zoo Dr.

Los Angeles, CA 90027-1498

(323) 644-6400

www.lazoo.org

The Los Angeles Zoo is one of the primary captive-breeding facilities for California condors. The zoo also prepares condors for release into the wild.

The Peregrine Fund

5668 W. Flying Hawk Ln.

Boise, ID 83709

(208)362-3716

www.peregrinefund.org

An organization focused on preserving endangered raptors and California condors. The Peregrine Fund has been a key player in the captive breeding and release of condors into Arizona.

The San Diego Wild Animal Park

15500 San Pasqual Valley Rd.

Escondido, CA 92027-7017

(760)747-8702

www.sandiegozoo.org

The San Diego Wild Animal Park is one of the primary captive-breeding facilities for California condors. The Wild Animal Park also offers public viewing of California condors at the Condor Ridge exhibit.

Ventana Wilderness Society (VWS)
PO Box 894
Carmel Valley, CA 93924-0894
(831)455-9514
www.ventanaws.org

A private conservation organization focused on the reha-bilitation and recovery of native species of wildlife to the Ventana Wilderness Area of central California. VWS has been an important contributor to the recovery of Califor-nia condors by releasing condors near the Big Sur region of California.

Website

U.S. Fish and Wildlife Service–Hopper Mountain National Wildlife Refuge (www.hoppermountain. fws.gov). This site provides a great deal of detailed infor-mation about California condor recovery activities and includes activities and information for children.

Video

Condor. National Audubon Society, 1987. Follows the saga of the decline and attempted recovery of California condors, including information on the behaviors and physical characteristics of condors.

ancient condors, 6, 7
Andean condors, 6, 27
appearance, 8

beaks, 9
behaviors, 10–12
black vultures, 6, 27
breeding
  in captivity, 30–32
  in nature, 12

California Condor Recovery
  Plan. *See* captive-breeding
  program
California Fish and Game
  Commission, 27
California gold rush, 17
captive-breeding program
  developed, 26–28
  locations of, 29, 36
  release sites of, 37–40
  success of, 28–29, 33, 36
  techniques used in, 30–32,
    34
carrion, 9
chicks
  in captive-breeding
    program, 26–29, 30,
    31–32, 34
  in nature, 12
Clark, William, 15
Cooper, James G., 22–23
courtship ritual, 12

DDT, 18, 20
de la Ascension, Antonio,
  14–15
diet
  of ancient condors, 6, 8

importance in nature of, 9
  types of food, 14
dominant birds, 11

Easton, Robert, 23–25
eating habits, 9
eggs
  in captive-breeding
    program, 30–32
  collection of, 18
  in nature, 12
Endangered Species Act
  (ESA), 25
explorers, 14–15
extinct condors, 6, 7
eyes, 8
eyesight, 10

family, 6
feathers, 8
flying, 10–11
foraging, 11

habitat
  loss of, 21
  protection, 36–37
  requirements, 13
heads, 8
hearing, sense of, 9–10
Hopper Mountain National
  Wildlife Refuge, 36–37

insecticide, 18, 20
intelligence, 11

Koford, Carl, 25

La Brea tar pits, 7
lead poisoning, 21, 34–35

Lewis, Meriwether, 15
life span, 13
livestock predator programs, 18
Los Angeles Zoo, 28, 29, 36

mating, 12
migration, 11

National Audubon Society, 25
National Wildlife Refuge System, 36-37
nesting sites, 11, 12
New World vultures, 6

Oregon Zoo, 36
organizations, 25, 26-27, 36, 38-39

Peregrine Fund, 36, 39
poaching, 35-36
poison, 18, 21, 34-35
population
  comeback, 40
  decline, 6, 14, 15-16, 21

ranchers, 18
range, 15-16
refuges, 22, 25, 36-37
reproduction
  in captivity, 30-32
  in nature, 12
restoration
  laws, 25
  organizations, 25, 26-27, 36, 38-39

sanctuaries, 22, 25, 36-37
  see also captive-breeding program
Robinson, Cyril, 23-25
roosting sites, 11, 12

sanctuaries, 22, 25, 36-37
San Diego Wild Animal Park, 28-29, 36
Sespe Condor Sanctuary (Sespe Wildlife Area), 22, 25
settlers, 15, 17-18
sight, sense of, 10
size, 8
soaring, 10-11
sport hunters, 18, 21

Teratornis incredibilis, 6
territory, 11, 14
threats
  to captive-breeding program, 32-33, 34-36
  previous, 18, 20, 21

U.S. Fish and Wildlife Service (FWS), 22, 26, 36
U.S. Forest Service, 25

Ventana Wilderness Society, 38-39
vultures, 6, 27

wings, 6, 8, 12
World Center for Birds of Prey, 29, 36

Greg Austin, U.S. Fish and Wildlife Service
Chandra David, Los Angeles Zoo
Jan Hamber, Santa Barbara National History Museum
Cindy Hoffman, U.S. Fish and Wildlife Service
Ronald M. Jurek, California Department of Fish and Game
Michael Mace, San Diego Wild Animal Park
Chad Olson, National Park Service
Sophie Osborn, The Peregrine Fund
Bruce Palmer, U.S. Fish and Wildlife Service
Andi Rogers, Arizona Game and Fish Department
Debbie Sears, Los Angeles Zoo
Kelly Sorenson, Ventana Wilderness Society
Denise Stockton, U.S. Fish and Wildlife Service
Michael Stockton, U.S. Fish and Wildlife Service

Dr. John E. Becker writes books and magazine articles about nature and wild animals for children. He graduated from Ohio State University in the field of education. He has been an elementary school teacher, college professor, and zoo administrator. Dr. Becker has also worked in the field of wildlife conservation. He currently lives in Delaware, Ohio, and teaches writing at the Thurber Writing Academy. He also enjoys visiting schools and sharing his love of writing with kids. In his spare time, Dr. Becker likes to read, hike in the woods, ice-skate, and play tennis.